HOME THROUGH BAGHDAD

22 JULY 2016

Dear BG Russo,

Thank you for the last 20 years of quietly reassuring and mentoring me, and even saving thy puppy from being blown off the parade field at Camp Niantic! All my best in your retirement - you will be missed! Yours

Dawn

HOME THROUGH BAGHDAD

DAWN M. WORKS-DENNIS

Outskirts Press, Inc.
Denver, Colorado

Home Through Baghdad
All Rights Reserved.
Copyright © 2010 Dawn M. Works-Dennis
V3.0

Cover Photo © 2010 JupiterImages Corporation. All rights reserved - used with permission.

Outskirts Press, Inc.
http://www.outskirtspress.com

ISBN: 978-1-4327-4407-6

Outskirts Press and the "OP" logo are trademarks belonging to Outskirts Press, Inc.

PRINTED IN THE UNITED STATES OF AMERICA

Table of Contents

CHAPTER 1

I don't know how I ended up in Iraq, and in the big picture, even less about what I was doing there. I don't know how to write a book. So while I am flipping back and forth in time, lost in thought, and I don't make any sense, remember, I don't claim to be an author. I have been writing my thoughts down for six years now, and really, I am just trying to get some things off my chest. You get to be my shrink, my judge, my intimate friend. Are you ready?

I started writing this while I was in Iraq, but I just can't seem to stop. I make myself nutty with the edits. For instance, it is Memorial Day weekend 2009, and I am rewriting the intro to this very short book for the twentieth time. My perception seems to change. I read my thoughts and think, "Wow, I think I can express myself better if I change this..." God only knows how many permutations this intro alone has gone through. I have lost count. So let me start with what I had six months ago, and I am telling you now that it won't make any sense. But, if I am ever going to finish writing this, I cannot go back and keep trying to make my writing better.

My husband was deployed to Tikrit in 2006, so I got a new puppy. But even with all the attention Pappy needs, I still have too much time on my hands. So, I write. Mostly this is sad and dark. That's because I'm depressed and drink too much wine.

But I guess I don't care. Everyone knows I drink too much, but who is going to tell a veteran to stop? I've earned the right. As long as I get out of bed and go to work (most days) then things are going well. Maybe I'll get around to telling you about Lester the butterfly and some other light-hearted tales from the desert, but probably not. War isn't butterflies and puppies, not tonight anyway.

I used to be a social worker but didn't adjust too well when I got back from Iraq. Let me rephrase that. I've adjusted perfectly. I've just lost a great deal of empathy for other people's suffering. Now I work full-time for the National Guard and plan to retire from the military. I had a different life once. Something separate from The War on Terror. I had a life that had nothing to do with war, and now it's war every day of my life. I don't get to live in oblivion, and sometimes wish I could get that back. Seriously, to have a day that I don't think about death and war, now that would be a good day. To have a night that I'm not drunk and crying, that would be a good night. You're probably thinking, "Jesus Christ, why doesn't she get some help?" I did. I even tried therapy. But all the therapeutic knowledge I have made me a bad patient. It's hard to counsel someone who already has all the answers from DSM IV. So, it's back to the wine and the tears. But telling my story is going to help, isn't it?

We weren't at war when I joined the military. So I give credit to everyone who has joined since we started tearing up the Middle East. There is nothing extraordinary about my military experience, not even the fact that I am a woman, or that I am a combat veteran. There are no trenches or defense lines to signify where combat starts and ends, and so there are tens of thousands of women who will come home from Iraq as combat vets. I'm not special, and isn't that sad too? I know there will be plenty of people out there who take a look at this book and say, "What the hell does she know about combat?" That's fine. I really don't give a shit what you think. The military gives me the "inner fortitude" to tell you that.

This story starts with redemption and I think it ends that way too. I joined up to save myself from a wreck of a life and came back to the same wreck. There are some illusions in the National Guard that are very tempting to the brokenhearted and rejected. But in the end, whatever you are trying to get away from, you'll end up with tenfold if you don't really get what the military is about. Sometimes, being part of a big machine, even a war machine, is the ultimate salvation. I think that's what I got. I got saved from my own microscope. To be honest, no one else gave a shit that I lost a job and wrecked a relationship, and looking back now, why the hell did I care either? Salvation. Lots of people get it at the altar. I got it in uniform.

I ran off to basic training at age twenty-seven with a destroyed ego and a desperate desire to be ignored. I didn't want any responsibility. I wanted to follow. I was spellbound by my drill sergeants. One of the most amazing things about the whole experience of basic training was to be around so many male role models who did not show any interest in me sexually, and who I wasn't trying to seduce. Which doesn't mean they didn't turn me on either. But flirting with a drill sergeant at Fort Jackson in 1997 just wasn't an option. I have read all the horrific drill instructor abuse reports that you have. But that wasn't my experience. My instructors were the good gods.

By age twenty-seven, all my professional experience had been with female social worker types. Wonderful, talented women. Remarkable women. The drill sergeants were my first glimpse into positive male power and influence since high school. That connection to men in uniform, and the way I can respect them like the women in my life, continues to this day.

After basic training and advanced individual training it was back to the life I thought I had fled. My boyfriend wanted me back so I went, and we got engaged. I did under-the-table housekeeping for cash, and I plowed ahead and finished my bachelor's degree in two semesters. Despite all the knee-jerk reasons for joining the military, when I tell you it was my salvation, I am not kidding. I came home on fire, and that fire is still burning twelve years later.

When I got back from five months of Army training in 1997, I realized that maybe I had a little more to offer than GI-ing the latrines. I have a good friend who I always enjoy reminiscing with about the early days of my career. MSG Madej likes to tell the story of me asking, "What the hell do I have to do to be in charge around here?" while I was holding a broom or some such humiliation. His direction was Officer Candidate School. That would show me the light. Boy, did it. The bliss of being lost in a formation was over. I went from being lost in the crowd to calling cadence. And I had no idea that crawling through goose poop on the parade field at Camp Rell could be so enlightening. Thank you, MSG Madej. Pain is temporary, glory is forever.

By the spring of 2002 I had gone from Private First Class carpenter mason, to First Lieutenant, Engineer Officer. I was singing in a band with my now fiancé, working on my master of social work degree, planning a wedding, and working professionally as a clinician. By all accounts, I had the world by the balls. September 11th 2001 had come and gone, and our forces were massing in Kuwait. Despite that immense buildup of power, I was simply proud to be in the Guard, and oblivious that I could be sent to war.

I wasn't really thinking about Iraq in the summer of 2002. With all that posturing and buildup my life had taken some drastic turns in eight months and I was pretty much only thinking of myself. I had brutally left my fiancé and was instead head over heels in love with an Army officer. I had left my good job as a clinician because I was now living with my brother and sister-in-law and couldn't keep up the commute. I never saw our mobilization coming. Not to Iraq. Not on the first wave. They were going to gas us and infect us with small pox?! Ho-ly shit! That is not why I joined the Army!

We received our alert on Valentine's Day 2003. What a maelstrom of fear and anger that followed. Not just for the soldiers but our families as well. There were seventeen year old kids in the unit, father and son teams, and before we even made it out of the States, more than one pregnancy. Somewhere in there, while I was freaking out, the blessed calm of resolve showed up. Have you ever heard the term "suck it up and drive on"? This is the crude and perfect motto of a soldier. Our Army trains us to do the shitty jobs no one else wants to. So I was ready to do what I had to, even though it was the complete unknown.

The morning we flew into Kuwait the temperature was ninety degrees by six a.m. With the flight and the time change we had lost twenty-four hours, and we were already counting the days until we could go back home. That was long before the tactics of our enemy would change, and "three-hundred sixty-five days of boots on the ground" became the new order. We were exhausted, hot and drooping. We had flown out of Fort Drum the day before wearing field coats. We had completed three months of cold weather training in lake-effect snow to go to the desert.

Wary of all the deadly threats of dehydration, I promptly sucked down three liters of water and spent the next two hours hitting the port-a-john every fifteen minutes. I learned to pace the water consumption because I feared the shitters and toilet crabs worse than dropping. By the end of the first week, though, I was drinking five liters a day and only using the johns every few hours. Synchronicity had been achieved.

Day four in Kuwait, I shave my head. Not GI Jane style, but an ugly number three buzz cut that sticks straight up like peach fuzz. I am liberated from my hair and slightly relieved from the heat, but immediately deemed a lesbian. Men are fools. I walk around feeling self-conscience for about a week, then realize that they are all still turned on because I am female, and if I am a lesbian, then it just fuels their girl-on-girl thoughts. I am antagonized for being "out of reg" with my buzzed head, and I just argue back that who really gives a shit when we are going into God knows what conditions…I'm a fucking warrior, so fuck off.

My shaved head makes me laugh, and helps me stage my own little war against "the man." This is real life, I might die in battle, and I refuse to be shamed because I look like I could be a lesbian. Strange how something so insignificant became such a debate. I'm not the only one who shaved my head. There were five of us that day, and we stuck together in the conviction that a shaved head made sense. And there were women from other units all over the base in Kuwait who looked and felt the same way.

Our shaved heads were just a glimpse into the coming months. A soldier's life from day to day is nothing like they produce in Hollywood. The world sees soldiers torn from their cozy nests and sent into battle, training and marching in perfect formation. In the real world, the battles are overshadowed by poverty and reduction to primitive living. Poverty is a fact. We are forced into it. The bank accounts back home grow, but we are condemned to live in the worst conditions in the most underdeveloped places on earth. Starting with the lack of plumbing. There is no steady stream of hot water, or any running water for that matter. For ha-ha's God throws in one-hundred-and-twenty-degree temperatures and wash water that smells like unrecognizable chemicals.

After a week the skin crawls and we have to force ourselves

to eat. I knew about poverty before the war, but now I *know* poverty. I've gagged on clouds of sand full of deadly particulate and had to squat in the middle of a road while camels and men walked by. I've pissed into a Pringles can, in the backseat of a Humvee, driving down the highway, because we couldn't stop for such a routine thing when we might take fire. The guys could always piss into a bottle, but it wasn't the same for the women. Before you say, "That's why women shouldn't be in combat," let me say, we sucked it up and drove on.

I've been under the leering, watchful eye of hundreds of men and male children who told me they would like to "fuck me" even while I was holding a loaded weapon in their direction. I know poverty. I know what it is to be a woman outside of America. I know what it is to have a baby held out to me by an Iraqi woman whose front door is busted in, and whose husband is zip-tied in the dirt out front. These are my snapshots. No different than what you see on CNN. Just kidding.

CHAPTER **2**

The medivac is landing again, kicking up a cloud of sand that will find its way inside, coating everything. We used to look up and wonder who it was this time. The medivac protocol, loss of life, limb, or eyesight. Back at Fort Drum I saw my first real medivac during an unreal training exercise. The red smoke, a captain running past me in full sprint. I cheered him on with a "hooah, sir" because the smoke was yet to come and because I did not know a soldier was in cardiac arrest. I had watched that bird lift off in the rain while snow and mud sucked at my boots. I fought back tears without knowing the soldier and wondered if it would eventually be one of mine.

The medivac site is across the street from our company area now. The routine landings dull my concern, and I just swear at the clouds of sand. The heat drives us outside to sleep. I curse the heat and curse the medivac for waking me up. That part inside that isn't pissed by the inconvenience still asks, "Who's hurt?" but I let it slip away.

I watch the newest cloud of sand drift through the compound. Soldiers are looking up now, covering their mouths and turning their backs like horses to the rain. The medivac, at least, does not hover over the compound like the Third Cavalry, observing us shower from one hundred feet. Some of the females wave up, their lean bodies an eternal source of power. I can't stop their waving. My demands for their modesty are met with twisted feminist logic: "Well, if the guys don't have to wear their shirts to the shower..." I chalk it up to youth. Few of them plan careers in the military and could care less if their breasts have been exposed to soldiers they might one day lead.

The showers have become a fixation. The guys in Horizontal Platoon had the foresight to pack plumbing all the way from Connecticut. Now in Iraq, they have built freestanding outdoor showers that we hook to the two-thousand-gallon water trailer at night. I look up at the stars while I shower, feeling sensual in the cool air, naked, clean. I haven't really seen my own body in months. This isn't the war of our fathers and grandfathers. We don't fight rats for our rations, or become combat ineffective from massive trench foot infections. I miss full-length mirrors and the simple pleasure of walking around naked. I slide my hands across my ribs and hips, enjoying the privacy, feeling the twenty-pound weight loss. My hipbones are prominent, my ribs individuals. I don't wave when the Blackhawk comes to hover. I watch its lights blinking and wonder if the crew are wearing night vision goggles.

I only started worrying about the NVGs after we issued them out to our own troops. I wonder how many of them are creeping around at night trying to get a glimpse of ass, or the latest couple having sex in the belly pan of a scraper. Sex and scrapers, love and war.

The medivac is lifting off and I briefly look up. The heat is maddening, eating our vitality. To sit is to sweat, to walk is to pour. In the midday heat the sweat drips off my hair and runs down my neck. Our Kevlars become torture devices, baking our brains inside their protection. We remove our flak vests, and our uniforms and T-shirts are soaked through. We can tell who has been working by the salt stains around the shoulder blades or outlining a bra. We can tell who has not been taking care of themselves when the salt stains start to look like waves. Soldier observation is a skill we can't afford to overlook.

The first week in Kuwait we force hydration and watch for some to drop with their weight and the heat. They drop on cue, suffering. We enhance their suffering, berating them for not getting in shape when they had the chance. This is no time for compassion. When one soldier ends up bagged in ice, his body unable to retain what he sweats out, we blame it only on him. "Suck it up. YOU ARE GOING TO DIE IF YOU DON'T DRINK." No one has dropped in months. No one has died either. The accidents have rolled through, our own medivacs and dust clouds. We all watch the liftoffs then.

CHAPTER **3**

Most of us have thought about shooting the dogs. Thin, wary creatures that sleep on top of the bunkers in the morning, and bark at the fence all night. We never think of feeding them. They are healthy enough to reproduce, feeding off our wasted meals ready to eat (MREs) at the dump. They have adapted to the desert. No matter how far out in the middle of nowhere we go, the dogs are there, listless and staring. We want to shoot them out of their misery. We want to shoot them out of that incessant barking.

We were reconning an enemy prisoner of war (EPW) camp at the far end of base when we saw the kicker. A small black pup leashed to concertina wire. She was sitting contentedly with the MPs, and while none of us approached her, our thoughts pounded like a heartbeat... "Want, want, want." The urge to nest and acquire includes puppies. A few days later a pup was magically found abandoned outside the compound. Soon after, the dogs began their midnight barking at the fence, one with clearly swollen teats. I shined my flashlight at them, too lazy in the heat to get up and throw stones. Their feral eyes glowed in the dark. Night after night they barked at the fence, demanding what was taken. Night after night I shined my flashlight and watched their glowing eyes, thinking of them as wild jackals or lions, circling our camp.

I can no more ignore the puppy than I can the barking. "Freedom" stumbles around the compound with her tongue hanging out and I have to stop. She nips too hard and goes for the ears if I pick her up. I pick her up anyway. I've looked through countless photos of war, and soldiers always acquire dogs. For all the bravado of war, and the constant trash talk about wasting Iraqis, I know no one who really longs for the kill. The puppy is tender. Her presence speaks of our combined need to care. She is constantly fondled and caressed, all of us falling over her and needing her affection. We were warned off the dogs here for all the diseases they carry, but were helpless to resist. All along the convoy routes, puppies are kept at the outposts, nurtured in defiance of the rules. At first we asked what would happen to Freedom when we leave, thinking she'd have to be shot. But as time goes on and we realize Americans are here to stay, we know she'll be taken in by the next rotation.

The sand cloud has moved on and I stub out my Newport. My throat hurts from smoking so much and breathing in hot air and sand for the last few months. But they help fight the boredom and break up the monotony. I sit in my chair with my ass soaked through with sweat, sipping on bottled water and smoking. Not so much as anybody else. But a lot. I sit in my chair and smoke and watch the compound. Soldiers doing soldiering, and soldiers sitting in their own chairs and smoking. The weather is no different today than it has been every day for the last few months. Hot, sunny, relentless. We sit and smoke and watch and bake in that relentless sun.

A fly lands on my arm. I flick my arm but the fly hovers and follows my arm back down, landing where it just sat. We perform this motion endlessly. The flies were slower in Kuwait. Maybe just as baked as we were. We sat in Kuwait and waited for our equipment to arrive for over a month before moving north to Iraq. The festival tents that housed us weren't yet air-conditioned and reached one-hundred-forty degrees during the day. Outside, the wind kicked up sandstorms. There was no escape. The heat would lull us down into midday naps. We'd wake soaked with sweat and feeling like we'd been beaten.

I was sent to the Port of Shuaiba to download our equipment. The tents were air-conditioned there, and I had to go outside to warm up in the middle of the night. When all the equipment was downloaded and I rejoined the unit, I spent three days re-acclimating to the heat inside the tents. I could barely function with the change in temperature, and know I looked weak and spoiled, despite the hard work at port. I had air-conditioning... enough in those days to raise jealousy and suspicion.

In the three months I've been in country I have only seen rain once. A sandstorm spit on us for about twenty seconds. Meanwhile I keep getting letters from home about all the rain back in my beautiful Connecticut. I imagine my return, sprawling on the grass, running my hands through the stream at Diana's pool, turning my face to the rain. Most likely we will redeploy in the dead of our New England winter. I will go home to the snow and cold. Since we left in winter, it will be almost two years before we see the green things we miss. Tom sends me photos of our fishing spots, the placid lakes and laughing brooks. They fuel my imagination and memories of home, everything I have to go back to. Mostly, though, I can picture our getaway spots without closing my eyes. I can see us on the banks, drinking merlot like drunks from a bottle, chasing down grasshoppers when we run out of bait. Always laughing. Always touching. I can barely stand the intensity.

The same memories that keep us going are our agony as well. I feel desperation and longing rise through my body in a sickening wave. I'm moaning inside. One moment I'm chasing a fly and watching the medivac. The next I am devastated. Hundreds of times a day my emotions roll my stomach. I force the good thoughts away and try to deaden myself to home. I'll get there when I get there. In the meantime, I pretend that this is my life and there was no life before it. I have always lived in Iraq. I have always worn the same clothes for a week. The weight of my M16 has always been on my back. These are good things. Things I want. Things I chose. I am a soldier.

There is a phenomenon that happens when soldiers leave home. We write. Every day there are mounds of letters in the US Snail Mail Pail addressed to home and countless friends who we reconnect with on a new level. These letters never speak about the pain. There is some unwritten rule about being upbeat and full of optimism. All the near misses and firefights and mortar attacks are somehow funny. Do we write with humor to save ourselves, or those back home? We cope. We write until our hands cramp and thank strangers and whole schools for their care packages. We hold on to civilization through the letters, letting people back home know that even in combat, we have good enough manners to send thank-you cards. Our parents raised us right. Even after invading a country and killing our foes, our letters signify that we are not barbaric.

No, we are not barbaric. There is no plundering. No mass rapes. No executions of the very young and the very old. Our war is different, humane. Saddam's army is reabsorbed into the general population without protest, ready to fight another day. The insurgent warfare has evolved into terrorist attacks that have killed more Americans than the combat that toppled Baghdad. Still, we fight with more honor and show more self-restraint. We would rather be leveling neighborhoods, and to hell with the women and children in them. But we don't. We just talk about it, fantasize about the utter destruction we are capable of, and then nothing happens but another IED attack that kills more soldiers. We are made impotent by our honor.

CHAPTER 4

Our company was given orders to move on to Ar Ramadi. Another base of rubble and mice and, now, the never-ending volley of outgoing artillery. We've come into the heart of the Sunni Triangle, further into combat. The medivac is no longer a nameless entity but Witch Doctor friends we pull security for on flights. They throw candy at us as they fly over, and hotdog right over the compound showing off. We wave up every time, many times a day, no longer bothered by the disruption and noise. The helicopters always pass over to the theme song from M.A.S.H. I hear the music in my head and I am secretly thrilled by the threat and the strength that helicopters represent. We have the sky secured and can blaze across the desert raining death and hellfire.

The artillery fire isn't bad either. It alternates between scaring the hell out of me and raising the hair on the back of my neck, to simple indifference. We learn to differentiate between incoming and outgoing, not always getting it right. I've gotten into full battle rattle at outgoing fire, and rolled over in bed at incoming. More indiscriminate attacks that could kill me where I lay. Usually I don't think about it at all, until there is another thundering boom that erases all thought. We cringe, we laugh, we howl like the dogs for lack of words to express our thrill or startle. We cope some more, and watch for the sky to light up with illumination rounds. The rounds come and go all over the place every few days. In between, I forget that we are under attack. Sometimes the rounds go out every hour all night. I get angry from the noise and hope that if I'm losing sleep, someone is dying.

The rains have finally come. They are not significant, and nothing like the biblical proportions we expected, but operations are still impacted. The water doesn't saturate the ground here due to the compacted clay and the top layer of moon dust. The rain simply gathers where it falls and turns our dustbowl of a base into a mud hole. We slosh through it and kick our boots against the buildings before we enter. Clumps of mud stick to the new paint three feet off the ground from the spray off our boots.

Just as the winter rains began, my platoon was sent to Habbaniya.

CHAPTER **5**

Habbaniya broke things up, gave the platoon a chance to practice some good ol' fashioned carpentry and brotherhood. Picture a broken-down, post-apocalypse amusement park, and you've got Habbaniya. In the first few days we explored the base and were chastised for "running in and out of buildings like looters." I couldn't help it. I was looking for the spoils of war, and for booby-traps, like any good soldier would under similar circumstances. We were freed from the oppressive watch of our own company, where I still took shit for shaving my head. I was a platoon leader again, and there was no way for my abusive commander to reach me now. We were "out of the loop" in the best kind of way.

We bedded down with Bravo Company, who weren't used to the pretty young females in the platoon and who saw my rank, before seeing my gender, and called me "sir" before they could think. We gave them lights with our generators from the first night, when they had been in darkness after sundown for a month. We bonded quickly in those days. We ran too. The guys lifted weights and I ran. I ran with Bear, a smart young sergeant. Thanksgiving has always taken on a new meaning after a five-miler in the light mist, with muck kicking up on my legs, and nowhere to shower. And that meal with fresh salad and turkey, in a warehouse that a week before housed pigeons and a ton of bat shit. My freedom from the commander for those six weeks was like being freed from prison. We also hurt. We had our hearts explode with grief and sadness. For those of us in Gen Con II, the war will always be about our losses in Habbaniya.

His hands were gone, but he kept waving them at his face, brushing at the bandages over his eyes. The mine had cauterized his forearms, blackened skin to the elbow. C* and C* were flat on their ass, bleeding everywhere, fragments of F*s hands caught on their uniforms. Soldiers were screaming, deaf from the concussion of the explosion, but more than that. Witnesses to the destruction of F*'s future in a single second. How does the mind wrap itself around a mutilated man, his blood, the shock of the real deal? Nothing can prepare the soul, not the carnage of movies or TV. When a man is down and the combat medics are in the zone, we stand back and direct security, watch the perimeter while keeping one eye on the gore. And still, we are never hit by the brunt force of our own mortality. We are soldiers. We are witnesses. We do not expect the man on the ground ever to be us. We only wonder what that kind of pain must feel like. We wonder what it would be like to have the men in Class A's at the door, to be the one with the loss.

Hard soldiers walked around in a daze after the mine. Weeks passed and everyone talked about the next missions, the latest cache, how bad the food was. No one talked about F* being in a coma at Walter Reed. No one talked because it was so present in their minds, and anyone could be next.

The Iraqis finished building the new partitioned barracks and everyone moved in, loud and clamorous in their new cribs, an atmosphere like a college dorm rather than a battlefield. I was immediately pissed off. I tossed at night and could hear the faintest play of CDs and TVs from the far end of the warehouse.

C* comes back from the field hospital. His pretty face is scabbed and his lacerated wrist is in a brace to keep the stitches from working their way out. He is in the land of the living. Physically sound, but I watch his eyes. They are beautiful. Round. Perpetually surprised. I watch for signs, touch him whenever I can, speak gently. He tells me about the day he was peppered with shrapnel. He had stepped around the very mine that F* picked up. The whys will drive us all crazy. No one will leave Iraq unscathed.

I have been in no firefights in Iraq. People have shot in my general direction, but I feel no real fear. I do not fear the bullets nor RPGs. We laugh about what bad shots they are. But the IEDs…that's another story. Every second of every convoy we clench our bodies, hyper vigilant to every rock pile, disturbed ground, piece of tire. I commute for hours at home without thought or preparation. The planning to convoy now takes days. We arrive exhausted from the stress of a two-hour convoy. I will my body and mind to relax while the HMMWV rattles down the road. We have been trained to open fire and obliterate anything hostile.

But there is no preparation for the IED. Rarely warning. I

relax and sometimes pray, realizing that at any second my face, my head, my life could be splattered over the driver without my ever knowing. Or splattered and dying of shock. Or splattered and surviving with little of my limbs intact. There is no way to make peace with this and so I do not try. I simply watch the road and everything around me. I purposefully work my way into the command of the convoys. Directing over the net to keep my mind busy and distracted.

I watch the desert go by mostly by sunlight, but sometimes under the moon. The sand flows by with only the visual disruption of blowing trash. I get manic, let my endorphins wash away the fear so that I can stay in the fight. I make light and laugh from my seat, but still expect every convoy to be a death march. There is one night convoy when I pray to God with the conviction of a child. I beg God to let us survive the night because I am the convoy commander, and it is my decision to be out after dark. It is the evening of September 10th, and I do not want to convoy on the 11th. So the desert goes by in the dark and I pray, and I am terrified that we are going to die and it will be my fault. Please God, please God, please God; don't let these soldiers die out here. Sometimes I think I'm still in a state of grace from all that praying. But I also think God and I are even for my being there in the first place.

Works in a routine sandstorm, Ramadi. September, 2003

Works stands watch as a Lioness on a raid in Ramadi.
Winter 2003

A typical night in Al Asad,
one of the guys on burn-out latrine detail.

Freedom, the puppy.
Al Asad, June, 2003

Iraqi woman on the convoy out of Iraq.
April, 2004

Members of GEN CON II and B Co Ist EN BN,
board up a tower in Habbaniya.
November, 2003

Rogue 26
Author's Call Sign & Humvee
April, 2004

CHAPTER **6**

When we got orders to deploy to Iraq, I blurted out that there was only one way we were coming home, and that was home through Baghdad. I don't know why those words occurred to me. The motto caught on, and was even written on our trucks as we convoyed north out of Kuwait.

Now we have come full circle. We were ten months into this fiasco and packing for home when we got orders to march again to Victory South. We are indeed going home via Baghdad, not just stopping in BIAP along the way. This is our last jump-off.

It all comes at a price. We all feel that we have paid enough, but the government seems to think there's still a little blood left in the 248th. More than one soldier has commented that we can't punch our ticket until one of us is dead. How can I argue with that when I have pretty much the same reaction? We have spent the last year in Saddam's backyard, and now for the last hurrah, we are going into the house.

Of course we're not going into the house for a cocktail party. Just to watch the yard from the windows. Running a base camp takes a huge amount of soldier power just for security. We're going to Baghdad to guard the perimeter and escort contractors, so the Brass can do what they do. That is what our little engineer company is reduced to. There are 120,000 soldiers in Iraq, and out of that who knows how many are out getting the bad guys. Most of us are just guarding the wire in the little Army cities we have built. That is the nature of this beast. We need huge numbers just to support our own mass.

Whole books have been written about the logistics of warfare. We have a deeper understanding of it from the front. It is no longer about getting fuel to the tanks to keep the forward edge of the battlefield advancing. It's about who is going to search and guard the shit-sucking truck so that some fucked-up suicide bomber doesn't blow it up and kill anyone standing within fifty feet. This is real. And if it isn't the truck, then it's the contractor we've been working with for the last six months who was just trying to get inside, maybe map out the post, and observe the rotation of security at the gate. This isn't the X-Files, but trust no one.

CHAPTER **7**

I can never look into the Iraqi night without remembering September 11th. There was that day when we all looked to the sky and collectively held our breath at the lack of air traffic. It was surreal, emotional, apocalyptic.

We own the Iraqi sky, and there is the same strange lack of air traffic. The helicopters come in low. The F-16s fly over at all heights depending on the mood of the pilots. Tonight they are in the stratosphere, and I watch their tandem afterburners slowly banking across the sky. I never know they are there until the sound catches up and the power of the sound draws my eyes. And then, as always, I remember standing in my backyard, looking to the sky and thinking that the world will never be the same. I remember the tears, crying, shamed for my emotions, but too devastated to stop.

This world will never be the same. How can it? We ignored the rise of violence in Afghanistan and fed the Taliban to appease our Oil Gods. The Taliban ignored education and reason to feed its Expansion Gods. Central Asia spent twenty years falling apart with the death of millions of people, genocide, starvation, and once again the use of religion to rationalize murder. We fueled it. By fueled, I don't just mean the war for Enduring Freedom. I mean that we fueled the hatred and the ignorance in the Middle East and Central Asia that have brought us across the world to the Middle East and Central Asia to die.

We fueled that hatred pouring funds into arms, by supporting warring factions like chess pieces. We are simply fixing what we helped wreck. We can all see cause and effect in two towers falling, but we didn't really know what we caused when we tried to keep the Soviets out of Afghanistan. We have no idea what we have done by occupying Iraq. Perhaps in twenty years we will have undone all we did with international policy twenty years ago. Whatever we do, soldiers are going to die...and that is just so unbearably sad.

CHAPTER **8**

I would take the rubble and mice over being warehoused once again. Garrison barracks are a prison of noise. At any moment, night or day, I can hear the crinkle of bottles being crushed, loud conversations, movies playing, laughter, shuffling feet, something dropping, a locker opening, a locker closing, microwaves dinging, doors slamming. My head aches and I become so angry I need to scream. I lie on my cot in a fury, until I remember to start counting backward, slowly, picturing my cliff by the ocean and only the sound of the waves.

My hair is blowing in the breeze, even though I shaved it off back in Kuwait. I am wearing a pretty little dress with the soft silk brushing my legs gently. The scratchy, yet comforting sea grass whispers and sways against my fingertips. *Nine.* I look out over the ocean and watch the swell of the waves, the rhythmic sound of waves washing in and out. A gull is gliding noiselessly above, close enough that I can see the slight smile of his beak. He catches my eye, tilts his wings, flies higher while he smiles. *Eight.* I see tall evergreens to my left, stretching back away from the ocean. A meadow lies before it, just tall grass and the wink of dragonflies and summer winged things. I can take a path through the meadow and into the woods, or walk a gently winding path down to the ocean. I breathe in the salty air, and the sun is tingling on my face. I breathe deeply while the sun warms and browns my skin. *Seven*.

Reality. Over a hundred cases of sexual assault have been reported in theater, soldiers raping soldiers. I am disgusted to learn that our psychological screening is so poor in the military that it appears we have even exported serial rapists amidst us. Early on I theorized that the women were safer in the combat zone than back home, where their husbands and boyfriends beat them, their ROTC/cadet brothers get them drunk and incoherent, and ex-lovers stalk and murder them. I'm sure statistically that I am still right. Most of the cases came out of Kuwait, where alcohol and drug use is more prevalent, and the soldiers don't walk around with weapons and ammunition. Maybe women should all be allowed to carry pistols on their hips back home.

I choose the path to the evergreens. My body feels strong and relaxed as I walk along. I am not strolling because I am fit and my body wills itself to move more quickly. I am lean and healthy and calm. I feel balanced as I cross the meadow, and only the soft sounds of birds and summer reach my ears. *Six*. Today was Diane's birthday and I forgot to email her. I reach the towering pines and enter the forest. The sun slants through the trees, sending rays errantly to the forest floor. My steps are muffled by the soft pine litter, and I can smell the sea, the grass, and the mixed relaxing aromas of the woods. There is a soft blanket of moss and I stop to sit and relax, my back against a giant oak that happened into this spot. *Five*.

And this is how it goes until I reach *one*, and I am relaxed, and the rage at my circumstances has passed. There is so much fury in our unit, at our leadership, at one another, but mostly at realizing we are prisoners. No one was angry being sent to Iraq. There was fear and trauma, but we forced ourselves to deal with these emotions and to do the best job we could, to bring everyone home alive. Now, after our redeployment has been stalled for over half a year, we feel trapped, misled, and full of rage. We have reached a point that getting through the next twenty-four hours is the only goal. We celebrate the coming of night, for another day has ended. Sometimes, we are exhausted just by breathing.

CHAPTER **9**

Today the rain is falling and I am still. I cannot forget the power of my deployment, and I continuously compare today with yesterday. Every time I say, "In Iraq things were blank, blank, blank," I wonder who I am boring. I am bored to hear others speak of it. My experience was briefly published (an early stab at this book) and I am a star amongst those who know me. I get some calls from those who were there with me. I touched some. Some still talk behind closed doors and say, "What does she know?" For some, it still comes down to me being a woman in an engineer unit and therefore, I must not have had a "real" combat experience. They say this from behind their desks, having never been in the desert themselves. They say this while still thinking that women can't be in combat because of our "cycles." You stupid bastards. I know you, but you still don't know the half of me.

I was in charge of a convoy that went horribly wrong. I will never forget nor forgive myself for the turn of events that followed. We all think that if we are going to die over there, let it be in combat. Yet most of our deaths are from accidents. We had gone on a convoy back to Kuwait from Al Asad. Four hundred miles back across Iraq for what ended up being toilets. Goddamn Americans and their porcelain gods. We sucked in hot air and sand, and after a two-day turnaround, we headed back to Iraq. We were dragging ass with heat exhaustion but had no choice but to push on. War is competitive. We were always driving on and challenged to get the missions done. Anything that wasn't done with haste was viewed as incompetence, even if it meant putting people and equipment at risk. That is combat.

Outside of Baghdad, a section of guardrail lay across the road. Our truck swerved to avoid it, which sent off a chain reaction, and the next thing I remember was the frantic call for "medivac, medivac, someone call medivac" over the radio.

My soldiers and I were damaged that day. We were not in direct combat, yet every sense of those words was recognized. Civilian Iraqis closed in, the air became stagnant, and fuel from the wreck seeped across the highway, threatening to catch fire and make the wrecks explode. An accidental discharge sent all of us into cover, and then my angry shouts—"What the fuck, get your fucking Kevlar on, where the fuck is your fucking Kevlar?!"—at a soldier who was standing there in shock at the carnage. A Marine convoy that we had been passing pulled security and over watch from the bridge ahead, and popped smoke for the medivac landing.

We had passed the Marines heading north on their first convoy into Iraq. They were laden with rucksacks and equipment and moving at forty-five to our sixty miles per hour. I had been riding in the cab of an M916 tractor-trailer because I was not provided a HMMWV, despite being the convoy commander and needing the mobility. When I heard the medivac call, we all pulled over and I jumped in with a HMMWV that was heading back to the collision. A soldier was trapped in the cab of the LMTV that had smashed into the HEMMT ahead. His face was spurting blood and he was incoherent...somehow alive. His legs were mangled and twisted in with the steel of the dashboard. The cab had collapsed around him like a viscous glove.

Marine major approached me from his convoy and asked me if I was in charge. "Is that your soldier?" he asked. I said, "Yes, he's mine, he's not in my unit, I only met him this week, but he's mine..." The major said, "Well, you need to get someone on that fuel spill before the truck catches fire and..."

The rest is lost in a series of images... I direct security, yell at people, pass out water, speak to the soldier and tell him to hang in there and that he is the toughest son of a bitch I have ever met. We improvise and pull the cab off of him with another truck and chains, as much likely to finally kill him as free him, if the chains let loose and the cab springs back.

My combat medic and the major amaze me. They flush him with IV bag after bag; they work on him and cradle him even as the cab is being pried from around him. They are covered by his blood and their sweat as the temperature reaches one-hundred-ten. There is no cover from the sun. I watch the curious civilians approach. They are getting too close; they are already trying to scavenge debris that has been thrown across the highway by the collision. I ask myself if these fuckers pried that guardrail across the passing lane on purpose...and what if they are hostile...are they smiling now at the injured American? Do they like to see his blood and hear his pitiful cries for help? I think yes, they enjoy this. Maybe in the same way I will eventually come to enjoy the thoughts of them dying.

My soldier is freed from the wreckage with one last scream of agony. He is broken in so many ways that I am still confounded by his living. I just want to cry. I want to cry all the time but can't. The medivac comes in and the purple smoke swirls. Dust is blown into my face and sticks in my sweat. The bird is now lifting up and my soldier has the chance to survive, but I am already wallowing in self-doubt, self-hate. Accidents aren't supposed to happen if you are a good officer and doing what you are taught. But the vehicles that collided weren't from my unit...they were from the unit we were convoying with... It's not my fault...

I'm disgusted with myself for the thoughts, but somehow comforted knowing that the vehicles were traveling too close... were they? Or was it the chain reaction that started with my own truck, and that I didn't slow down the convoy passing the Marines...if I had slowed down... What if I had radioed, "Slow down, rail across the road," would things have gone differently? I blame myself for that accident. I don't even try to make excuses. I waited for a reprimand...for a letter in my file...for anyone to tell me what a sorry excuse for an officer I was. It never came. I drove on knowing I was changed.

Two years later I find some closure from the unit out of South Carolina that we traveled with, the 122ND EN BN, our parent unit at the time of the accident. Their command sergeant major (CSM) has forwarded the announcement for the Valorous Unit Award our unit received under the Third Cavalry Regiment, and it is again forwarded to me by email. At once I am in touch with the CSM, and my first return email question is *How is that soldier?* He is still at Walter Reed.

I don't know why I'm not held accountable. Maybe I torture myself enough, without the military having to tell me what a failure I am. The soldier grants me reprieve. We email, too difficult to speak. I speak to others. They remember me being strong and sane and commanding of the convoy and the accident scene. They give me credit and respect for how I handled it. I can't give myself that credit and, even with closure, feel the burden of guilt.

CHAPTER **10**

I don't remember what I was doing when I was told that CPT A* was dead. I had a crush on him. He was a gentleman who loved his wife, and never made a pass at me. I was the only woman around him for months, and he never made a pass at me. He was one of those safe guys who made me feel human, like a competent person, and not an imposter or a piece of meat. I think about finding his parents in Rhode Island; they're practically next door. But how do you show up on someone's doorstep and say, "Hi, I knew your son in Iraq before he was killed by the insurgents. He was a good man and I still think about him all the time." Where do you take the conversation from there? Truth is, CPT A* gave me hope. He renewed my faith in what an officer could be, and needs to be, and then he was gone. We openly wept at the memorial service. Maybe I did more than others because I am just a girl and it was okay. I still weep. Another snapshot.

There were others who died in that set-up as well. Five beautiful men in all. Their Hummer rolled over an anti-tank mine. Today, there are Hummers all over the roads in America, so cool, so status-oriented, brightly colored, and fun...all I see is death. I see the fuel consumption, while we are at war for oil. I see a tarp pulled back from a vehicle with blood-soaked seats and the tires blown off. Just a twisted hulk of steel and five dead men. I see bodies sliced in half by shrapnel and ball-bearing-packed devices, hanging on to life, coughing blood. I just don't have any affection for Hummers anymore.

CHAPTER **11**

Now it's 2008. I have been home for four years. It gets harder and harder to go back...to come here. Part of me gets more honest. Part of me keeps burying things deeper. I think it's time to tell you about Lester the Butterfly. Lester flew through the window of my HMMWV on our way out of Iraq. We had been on the road for two days and were approaching the border of Kuwait. We had the usual shit from convoys, blistering heat, MREs, feeling like you would crap or piss your pants for mile after mile. Knowing your kidneys and bladder would never be right again. Then sleeping on your vehicle or a cot under the stars next to your vehicle, while the desert wind violently kicked dirt into your eyes, ears, and mouth, and the sand fleas made your skin ripple with bites.

Lester brought me the most bizarre sense of hope and calm. He landed on my hand, which rested across my rifle. He sat there against the wind, with no reason for being there. He (or she?!) rode with me for miles across the desert. I took a picture. Such a whimsical distraction from the final death march out of Iraq. There is nothing more to Lester. I just appreciated, and will never forget, the moment of calm I had with another creature that was blown in and rested in the most hostile of places.

April 2004 we were finally given orders to redeploy. We

were staged in Baghdad for our last convoy out of Iraq. We were trying like hell to get out of Baghdad, but we ended up stalled for three days. With our luck, insurgent activity was so high, no convoys could leave Victory South unless on combat missions. In the meantime we stocked the trucks, and did pre-combat checks and inspections, and waited for the go-ahead to leave Iraq.

Was that during Easter? I don't remember. But Easter happened. My platoon was tasked with guarding Slayer Tunnel. This tunnel originally allowed access to the base, and many people apparently did not know that it led into our base camp. We spent six hours laying an elaborate trip wire system and setting up crossfire. I emailed home with my usual war humor about the Easter Bunny coming through the tunnel. Funny thing is that some poor son of a bitch did drive through it...and I still laugh to imagine all those flares going off around some unsuspecting local.

Baghdad was different in many ways. There were six miles of interior road to run; I know this from the first and only 10K I have ever run. Peaceful, beautiful lakes, with the royal palaces sitting bombed in the middle. Special Forces parties. Rockets launched over our gate...watching those incoming contrails and realizing there was no place to run. My moments of absolute terror were few in Iraq. Baghdad claims one of them. Incoming rockets in broad daylight...hard to judge distance... projection...angle of descent... I was breathing heavy and realizing again that death was imminent. This time I didn't pray.

There was warehousing again. Stuffed into hardened buildings with sheets hanging between the bunks like a shantytown. The prison of noise. Walking 200 feet and down two flights of stairs to take a piss at night…half the time in the building…and when the insurgents blew the right pipes… back to the port-o-johns. Hot indoor showers with drains that clogged with Band-Aids, hair, and soap scum and ran over into the changing area. Filth. Clean, filthy showers. Oh, the blessings of running water.

Work. Run. Eat. Sleep. I'm in the chow hall late one night. I had run and gone to dinner late. Brigadier General Formica and his entourage arrive and he politely asks if he can dine with me. I am thrilled to get some positive attention! I sit there basking in the presence of a One Star. My rifle, Kevlar, battle vest and flak vest lying against the wall behind me. The same overcooked crap in front of me. We chat and discover we both hail from Connecticut. Then we discover that BG Formica and I happen to know the same restaurant down in Niantic. He lets me know that when I get back home to Connecticut, I need to visit his brother at Flanders Fish Market and get a free meal.

When I do get home about four months later and head to the restaurant, Tom and I get that free meal like we are part of the family. Mr. Formica has now gone on to become First Selectman Formica, and we see each other about once a year in social passing. He always remembers me. We always share that memory. Our affection, like so many Americans, comes from a small but significant connection through the military.

Is there a way to end this gracefully, or describe the

redemption I said this story might end with? I don't know. Maybe there is no redemption after all. I've been home for over five years now and I've read through this a hundred times, editing, reading out loud, always with a glass of wine to numb the impact. Always trying to get it right, and maybe get through to someone, anyone, that combat isn't what it is cracked up to be. I am not redeemed. Service in the military is damaging. It hurts, but it also transcends. Whatever I felt I needed to prove in this life…I feel I proved enough in Iraq to see me through.

CPSIA information can be obtained at www.ICGtesting.com
Printed in the USA
BVOW02s2149140914

366784BV00001B/1/P